Moments, Memories, and Experiences

Live,
Love,
Laugh

Moments, Memories, and Experiences

SHANNON STEMLEY

Moments, Memories, and Experiences
Moments, Memories, and Experiences / Stemley, Shannon / Non-Fiction / Self-Help

ISBN: 978-0-578-777146 (print)

Table Of Contents

Acknowledgments

There are many people I would like to thank for helping me make the concept of my book a reality. First, with a sincere, grateful, and humble heart, I want to thank God for placing the idea of writing in my spirit and then seeing the mere idea come to fruition. I now realize every trial and tribulation prepared me for this manuscript and the many things yet to come. I walked this journey—as I do every journey—as a vessel and servant of God, ready to do His good works. Words can't describe how incredibly proud I am of myself for actually bringing this idea to life, but it could not have happened without God and my support system.

I have to thank my mom for her encouragement, love, support, and great vision that extended far past my own of what this book could become. I thank her for continually pushing me to see not just any vision but one beyond my thinking. Thank my god-sister and her husband, Sheila and Dee, for their constant encouragement, advisement, love, support, and care. I thank them for being there to review and provide feedback every step along the way, helping me make sure I gave my best and presented myself and my book in the best light.

I thank my children, my heartbeats, for being my motivation, inspiration, editors, proofreaders, and so much more (smiles). I thank every woman in my family because it is your grace, strength, dignity, integrity, values, morals, sassiness, and love that has helped me sustain and persevere. I also want to say how grateful I am for everything I've gone through—every heartbreak, every unfairness I suffered, every unkind word, every word of doubt, every word and action meant to break me because without those which the enemy sent to distract and destroy I would not have found myself, my way, God, or healed.

Shannon Stemley 7

"FREE FROM THE STRONGHOLDS OF UNTOLD STORIES, AND TRUTH IS THE LIFE I SEEK TO LIVE."

—SHANNON STEMLEY

"LORD, PREPARE ME FOR WEALTH, PREPARE ME FOR LOVE, AND PREPARE ME FOR GREATNESS."

-SHANNON STEMLEY

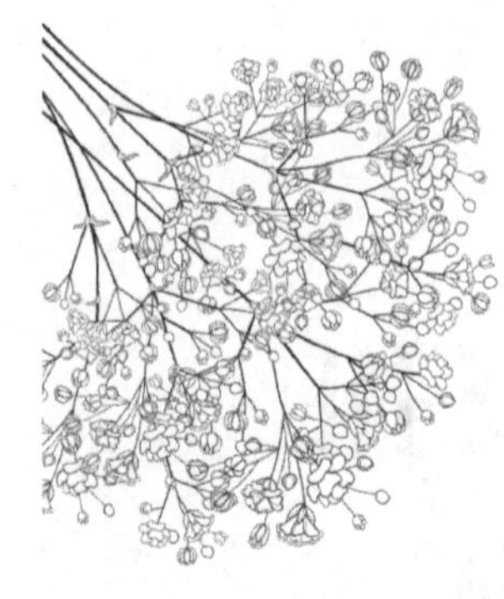

"SHE IS CLOTHED WITH STRENGTH AND DIGNITY, AND SHE LAUGHS WITHOUT FEAR OF THE FUTURE."

-PROVERBS 31:25 NLT

Hey Y'all!

Just life... This book is a collaboration of my experiences and innermost thoughts tolet other women know they aren't alone in their way of thinking or feeling when it relates to love, hurt, heartbreak, healing, and self-love. I, too, at times, have felt like no one could or would understand me. Over time, through casual conversation with women I've met, some in passing and others who I've been lucky enough to keep around, I learned I wasn't alone. In fact, I discovered most women had experienced some of the same things I had. I also learned I wasn't alone in my way of thinking, feeling, and/or how I interpreted those emotions.

There once was a time when you could not have paid me to talk openly about certain things I had gone through, especially those things concerning my relationships. Like many women, I was terrified to share my story. I was full of shame, embarrassment, hurt, and confusion. I felt judged, and I lacked everything you can think of that starts with the word self in fear of exposing parts of me that I wanted no one to see. I never thought I would be as comfortable as I am now, sharing my life and such vulnerable moments with others.

As I was going through my divorce, things changed. I changed, and slowly I became comfortable with sharing my story. While having a conversation with a close family member, I can recall her telling me not to be afraid of sharing my story because I never knew who I could be helping. I'm not afraid anymore to be completely open and raw about my past, thoughts, or experiences. I'm no longer fearful of what people will think or have to say. I love the woman I've become and the woman I'm growing into.

I embrace the trials and tribulations I have gone through because I wouldn't be who I am today without them. The heartbreaks, hurtful experiences and struggles, and life lessons pushed me into an extremely uncomfortable place of self-awareness. That self-awareness helped me see parts of me that needed some work—to see the brokenness, the ugliness, and weakness. That self-awareness is what set me on the path to wanting to heal, grow, and become the woman I desire to be… GOD desires for me to be. Everyone heals differently. The steps one takes to elevate themselves, find themselves, and love themselves look different for each individual.

Many times, we think one good cry session will fix everything. We don't know there will be hundreds of cry sessions, periods of self-isolation, screaming, anger, and uncertainty. There will also be times when you question yourself, battle some ugly demons, have tons of ah-ha moments, and a whole lot of praying before that "Queen B" attitude kicks in. My healing and self-love journey included advice from a life coach, confiding in one individual I trust with my soul, a host of bible scriptures, quotes, and affirmations. I read and spoke to myself daily, reminding myself WHO I am and WHOSE I am.

This book is comprised of those exact bible scriptures, quotes, and affirmations, as well as a few very personal thoughts, feelings, and life experiences throughout varying relationships. I hope they can help you as they have me on your journey to healing and love to becoming an altogether better version of you. Healing, strengthening your core, and finding that inner happiness and joy is not an easy journey, but it must start with you. Enjoy, love bugs!

Live,
Love,
Laugh

"I'M FIXING ME BECAUSE I RECOGNIZE THIS IS WHERE THE PROBLEM STARTED."

-SHANNON STEMLEY

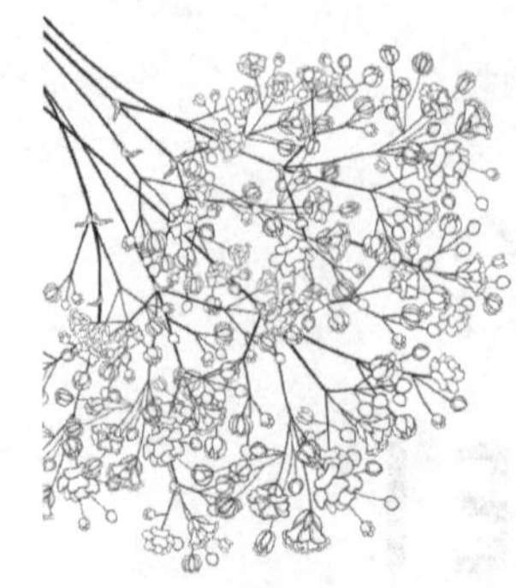

"YOU WORRY LESS
WHEN YOU KNOW
THE WORD OF GOD
AND
TRUST THAT HE'S
GOTCHA!"
–SHANNON STEMLEY

"WAKE UP EVERY DAY
READY TO BE A
BLESSING INSTEAD OF
ALWAYS LOOKING TO
RECEIVE THEM."
-SHANNON STEMLEY

Self-Reflect

Realization # 1

WHY. AM. I. NOT. ENOUGH?

My heart is broken. I feel sad, hurt, and confused. I'm constantly questioning myself, why. Why am I not enough?

When you have been good to someone and given them the best parts of you, you don't expect them to turn around and treat you like nothing; it is a horrible feeling. I was good to my ex-husband. I genuinely cared and had an interest. I supported him and wanted to see him reach his goals and become the best version of himself. The problem is, I gave so much of me trying to help him become his best that I literally lost pieces of myself in the process. I was losing all that made me my best.

The amusing part of it all is that it was never reciprocated. I felt like a complete fool for wanting to help someone who had no desire in their heart to do anything for me. I sat on my sofa, questioning my actions, and trying to understand why it bothered me so much. I recalled recent conversations, and I asked myself, "What is it you're afraid of?" I needed to know what negativity within compelled me to want to hold onto something that was clearly not for me. As I sat in that moment, in those emotions, I grabbed paper and pen and began to answer, writing, "My fear is…"

Then I closed my eyes and said, "Moment of truth." I had to let go of fear and shame and answer the question honestly, which by the way, was extremely difficult to do because no one wants to see themselves embarrassed and afraid. Deep breath in, deep breath out, and then I wrote.

My fear is:

- Rejection.
- Not being good enough.
- Not being loved.
- Not being protected.
- Not being wanted.
- Not being attractive enough to keep a man.
- Not being intellectual enough.
- Not being a ride or die by society's standards and definition.
- Not being curvy enough.
- Being cheated on again, being lied to some more, and being used.

Considering my list, the worst thing ever is feeling like you've been used or made a fool. How had I allowed this yet again? How did I allow another guy to get that close to my heart—to me—and to make me feel like I wasn't enough or had done something wrong by being me? I began to wonder the very thing most women do when we feel rejected.

I wondered:

- How could he not love me as good as I was and after all I did?

- Who does he think he is to treat me that way?

The truth is, he was exactly who I accepted him to be in my life. I allowed mistreatment and unhealthiness; I set the tone for what I now resented. This was all my fault for not standing my ground and setting healthy boundaries from the beginning. He treated me how I taught him to treat me by what I made acceptable. My fear of saying the wrong thing because I was afraid of running him off had gotten me here. I knew exactly what my standards were and what I wanted in a man, but I did a poor job at standing firm with it. Again, I asked, how did I allow this to happen to me yet again.

Knowing now that people treat you how you teach them to treat you by what you make acceptable, I also had to admit loneliness had also brought me here like every other woman who struggles with doing what's right versus settling for a little attention. Was that bullcrap version of attention worth the insecurity I felt after realizing how plain-out foolish and blind I had been? Having to sit myself down on my own sofa and ask the hard questions I daily avoided because I hoped no one ever found out what really goes on inside of me is one of the hardest things I had to do. So, you can only imagine how tough it was to put it all into this book for the world to now know.

I developed multiple insecurities through each relationship and situationship I partook in because I had not done a good job at standing up for me. I had not done a good job of sticking to the boundaries I set for myself either. I had not done a good job of knowing myself and loving me unconditionally. Nor had I done a good job of valuing myself and knowing my worth. Most importantly, I had not allowed God to take his position within my relationships.

Live,
Love,
Laugh

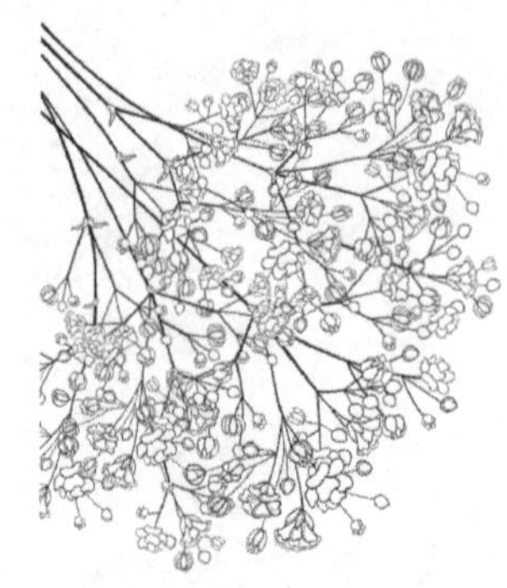

"BE FORGIVING. BUT DON'T BE NO FOOL."

-SHANNON STEMLEY

"YOU ARE ALTOGETHER BEAUTIFUL, MY LOVE; THERE IS NO FLAW IN YOU."

-SONG OF SOLOMON 4:7 ESV

"SOMETIMES, GOD TAKES YOU THROUGH AN UNCOMFORTABLE SHIFT TO GET YOU TO A COMFORTABLE PLACE OF BEING."

–SHANNON STEMLEY

Self- Reflect

Realization #2

My entire life, I have been this super-strong person who never took crap or succumbed to the pressures of life or its obstacles. So why should this be any different?

I know now, and I knew then that I'm better than what I allowed and accepted from people who weren't worth any of my time. I deserve so much more, but like many women, I still held onto the idea of what I wanted a relationship to be despite knowing this. I held onto the idea of what I wanted him to be and refused to let him go.

I had a stronghold and an unhealthy soul tie that I had no clue how to break. The crazy thing is that although I knew what I deserved, I also knew he was not what I genuinely wanted. He was inconsistent, nowhere near dependable, extremely immature, one of the biggest procrastinators I know, lacked every ounce of effort, and made absolutely no time for me. The only thing he had to offer me was some "good-good," if you follow.

So, what was it? It was everything all women want and fall victim to. For example, I took whatever little attention he offered as opposed to having no attention at all. It was just having someone to talk to. It was feeling like I had to give him the benefit of the doubt in hopes that the better version of him would soon prevail. It was sex. It was not holding myself to my own standards and making sure I adhered to the boundaries I created that were meant to protect me and my heart. It was wanting to believe that he loved and respected me enough to never hurt me. It was wanting to believe that somehow, I meant more to him than any other female. It was believing that if I hung in there long enough, being patient and supportive, he would eventually see my worth and know I was the one. It was his manipulative way with words that pulled me back in every single time. It was literally not respecting and loving me better than I did. It was not waiting on God and listening for His direction and discernment. It was not trusting God and allowing Him to be God. **It was loneliness—** sex and loneliness, foreboding spirits that know how to use our insecurities and fears against us.

What I learned was to trust God. No relationship is perfect. Know that if a man wants you, you will know it; if he doesn't, you will always be confused. I learned some people can fall in love with the *benefits* of you and *not you*. I also learned I had failed myself every time I ignored my gut, fearing I was thinking too much. I learned we really do teach people how to treat us by what we allow as well, and that my boundaries and standards were God's protection.

Live,
Love,
Laugh

"PAY ATTENTION TO HOW PEOPLE TREAT YOU. NO MATTER WHAT THEIR WORDS SAY, THEIR ACTIONS WILL NEVER LIE."

-SHANNON STEMLEY

"GO WHERE YOU ARE CELEBRATED, NOT TOLERATED."

-MIKE MURDOCK

(ONE OF MY GODSIS FAVORITES)

"THE HEARTFELT COUNSEL OF A FRIEND IS AS SWEET AS PERFUME AND INCENSE."

-PROVERBS 27:9 NLT

Self- Reflect

God's Lesson #1

Never stop being a good person because of how a person, undeserving of your goodness, treated you. Instead of seeking revenge, stooping to their level to make them feel how you felt, try to explain or express. Stay strong, keep your cool, and stay calm; then walk away knowing God has your back. Trust me, *God don't play about His children.* All your good deeds won't go unnoticed, not even by the person who hurt and/or wronged you. How poorly someone treats others is a direct reflection of how they feel about themselves, not you. I'm too blessed to try and hurt a person the way they hurt me. That takes too much energy, time, and I have too many seeds of good sown to add weeds. Believe me when I say, *you reap what you sow.* Sow your good seeds and let God do what He does best.

"GOOD OR BAD, PEOPLE WILL NEVER FORGET HOW YOU MADE THEM FEEL."

-SHANNON STEMLEY

"IT'S HARDER TO FROWN WITH A SMILE."

-SHANNON STEMLEY

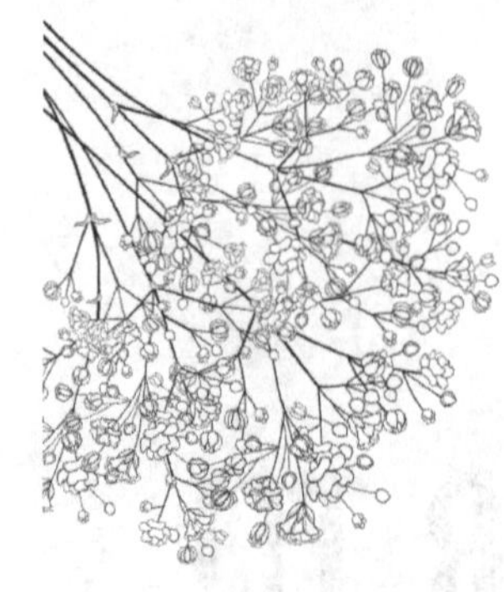

"TAKE DELIGHT IN THE LORD, AND HE WILL GIVE YOU YOUR HEART'S DESIRES."

-PSALMS 37:4 NLT

Self - Reflect

Live,
Love,
Laugh

Hurt

Every woman experiences heartache, brokenness, hurt, pain, disappointment, letdowns, confusion, setbacks, and situations that shatter and shake her spirits on a level that one could never explain. We try to couple those feelings and emotions with love, laughter, and positivity. We embrace any and everything to remove those unwanted feelings.

Men don't understand how their actions affect women beyond the surface and physical. Women are naturally emotional creatures. If you're like me, when you attach yourself to someone, give yourself to someone, allow yourself to love someone, you do this with every single part of you. *I love hard, and I hurt harder* is a phrase I like to use in describing how passionate I can be in and about love. I do everything with an extreme amount of passion, so that hurt—boy, that hurt—hits like something indescribable.

You begin to analyze everything right and wrong within you. You question every thought, conversation, action, and motive. You begin to ask, "Am I good enough? Am I worth it? Did I move too fast? Did I move too slow?" Nothing hurts like having to accept that someone really does not give a crap about you. **That hurts!** That hurt then turns into a rage-filled outburst, for some... busted car windows and slashed tires.

(Y'all know who you are, lol.) Like songstress Monica sings, "Kicking down doors and smacking chicks," lol. *Um-hm, y'all know exactly what I'm talking about.* I don't care what anyone says; that's some painful stuff to heal through.

I discovered that allowing myself to feel the hurt and pain instead of masking it or trying to cover it with other feelings, helped me heal. I permitted myself to feel however I wanted. I didn't put any mental energy into thinking about what anyone thought of the emotional roller-coaster I was on. *Affirmations are the bomb!* I discovered that speaking affirming words to myself daily helped me remember who I was. Speaking affirming, uplifting, and encouraging words to myself boosted my confidence. When I added prayer, reading mybible, and stepping into the presence of God, my healing elevated to another level because I was able to forgive not just the people who hurt me but myself as well.

When I began to talk about my thoughts and feelings with mentors, life coaches, and trusted people, I learned self-control, which taught me how to not operate from an emotional place but instead to let the smoke (feelings) die down until I can operate with a clear mind. For me, the questions became, what am I going to do with this hurt, and how am I going to let this define me. When I began to answer those questions, I realized I didn't particularly appreciate that I had allowed someone else to have that much control over my feelings, thoughts, or actions. I realized I did not want to be defined by my hurt anymore, and I took back control of me.

"BE CAREFUL WHO YOU HURT. SOME PEOPLE PRAY IN REAL LIFE AND WHEN THEY'RE HURTING AND CRYING, LIKE ANY FATHER, GOD STEPS IN TO PROTECT."

-SHANNON STEMLEY

"FOR GOD GAVE US A SPIRIT NOT OF FEAR BUT OF POWER AND LOVE AND SELF-CONTROL."

-2 TIMOTHY 1:7 ESV

"DON'T THROW THE BABY OUT WITH THE BATHWATER."

-ANONYMOUS
(ONE OF MY GODSIS FAVORITES)

Self-Reflect

Don't Overthink It

If you know me well, then you know I'm a thinker, and I process everything. When I started my journey to heal and grow, I was forced to tackle how I overthought certain things. Overthinking had become my enemy. It was causing me to self-sabotage in ways I didn't even understand.

I realized my overthinking was me trying to control my dating life's narrative and outcome and other areas of my life. This need to control was due to the hurt I suffered in previous relationships. It was unhealed parts of me I had punished others with too. I think I had developed a form of post-traumatic stress from all I had gone through and experienced in life. Now, at 36, I overthought every situation because I was trying to make sure no one had the opportunity to hurt me ever again.

As a preventative measure, I tried to make sure I saw the signs and caught anything that mimicked the bad. I was trying so hard to recognize all the red flags and signs I missed in previous situations that I was allowing this to ruin the good in present situations. For me to control the overthinking and to pretty much stop it and heal, I had to talk about and feel the feelings I had suppressed for so long about any hurt, pain, uncertainty, insecurities, disappointment, failure, rejection, etc. This part was not easy. Like, let's be real. Who enjoys having to face and admit they're a mess? That they're the problem sometimes?

I spent many days crying and sometimes screaming to release and free myself of any strongholds my past had over me. I wrote those feelings out. I began to read through my bible and comb through my favorite scriptures. I wrote down all my favorite quotes and affirmations to remind me of who I am and whose I am! Thus, creating this book of my thoughts, feelings, favorite scriptures, quotes, and affirmations. Doing this helped me through my healing process.

It helped me to:

- Feel peace.
- Find comfort in knowing who I was and being
  okay with not being perfect.
- Quiet my mind when the spirit of overthinking,
  deception, and confusion tried to come in.
- Find peace in just being a perfect imperfection and
  allowing things to flow.

Live,
Love,
Laugh

"THE HISTORY OF WHO I AM LIES IN THE PAST AND IS ONLY MEANT TO GUIDE ME THROUGH THE PRESENT AND FUTURE."

-SHANNON STEMLEY

"MANY ARE THE PLANS
IN A PERSON'S HEART,
BUT IT IS THE LORD'S
PURPOSES THAT
PREVAILS."
    -PROVERBS 19:21 EIV

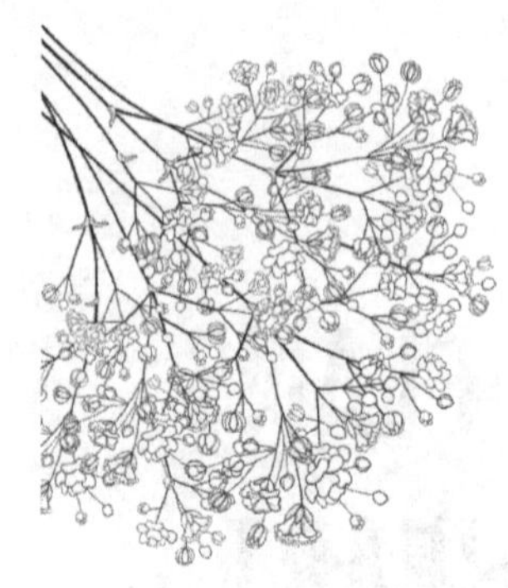

"GOD WILL ALLOW YOU TO
FOOLISHLY KEEP GOING BACK
TO THE WRONG PERSON
SO THAT YOU ARE COMPLETELY
COMFORTABLE WITH WALKING
AWAY AND LETTING GO."

-DEDRA STEMLEY

(MY MAMA)

Self- Reflect

Damaged Goods

Date singles! Date because that's the only way you will really know your standards and what you like and dislike. For me, dating was frustrating and too much work. By the time I was single again, I was a divorced, 33-year-old mother of three. Who has time for that? I cringed at the thought of having to get to know someone and them me all over again. At one point, I put my full focus and attention on my children, always using them as an excuse for everything. Then, I decided not to let all this goodness go to waste. *Ha!* So, I began dating!

I can't lie; I came across both fools and some good guys. I don't date like most people, so I quickly realized I wasn't a serial dater and decided to date one guy at a time versus five. I know what I like and what I want; however, my thing is this: if I find that I like a guy, then I put my time and energy into that **one**. I believe that *yes,* you can hang out and converse with multiple people, but for me dating one person at a time was more than enough stress. Let me tell you, when I was out here trying to pimp, I was messing the game all up. My mama even told me I was tarnishing her name, lol. I was forgetting what I had said to who and calling folks the wrong names. Not a good look at all! It was too much to handle, and I didn't have time for all the drama that each guy brought. *Nah... I'm good.* (I'll stick to one, and if I don't like him, well on to the next.)

I also feel you shouldn't be giving the same energy, time, effort, attention, consistency, and affection to every single person you're talking to or dating. It wasn't until I got serious with two specific guys that I realized I had some more healing to do. During and after my divorce, I chose to attend therapy because, honestly, my relationship with my ex-husband was horrible. It was full of emotional, mental, verbal, and sometimes physical abuse. My relationship with him had broken me in ways I didn't even realize until it was time to date again.

While I praised God daily for removing me from that situation, I was aware I needed some self-work. I was also aware that sometimes the problem was me. I assumed all the tools my therapist had equipped me with and all the releasing of emotions during that time had healed the hurt and brokenness within me. It wasn't until I went through my breakup with guy one that I noticed something lingering. I refused to open the wound of hurt he had caused and deal with what I felt. Still, I tried to apply all the techniques learned years before in therapy to move swiftly past that situation.

A year later, I found myself in another relationship with a different guy. I realized after a year into it how unhealthy and toxic it was. When dealing with guy two, I noticed several times throughout my relationship with him where I would react to certain things in a manner I wasn't pleased with. No, I wasn't busting windows or slicing tires, but he was a master manipulator, and he was full of game. I did what all females have done at some point; I drove by to make sure he was where he said he was. That, My Love, was an insecurity I developed from my past failed relationships— relationships that ended due to the lack of trust, honesty, and faithfulness. Every time I did a drive-by, he was not where he led me to believe. I would immediately go off and **be done**. The problem was, I was never done. He always found a way to pull my silly self right back in. *We've all been this stupid, so don't feel bad.*

Another of my toxic traits in this relationship was that I would never just say how I felt about his actions or words at the moment. Often, I would wait until things accumulated, then explode and cause him to look at me like I had lost my whole mind. I was bringing up things I should have addressed the moment they happened. Homeboy never took accountability or responsibility for anything he did. (Or at least not directly with me.) When confronted about his actions and behavior, he would always find a way to say it was my fault that we were at odds for reacting (or over-reacting) how I did. He never said, "I'm sorry" or "I was wrong," or "I take full accountability for my part." *Nope. Never.*

He lacked the understanding that everything had a cause and an effect. I didn't understand then that those moments of outburst and blinded stupidity needed to happen so that I could see the parts of me that needed working on and healing. Had none of it occurred, I would have never gotten to the point of self-reflection, self-healing, and self-awareness that I did. For so long, I assumed the therapy I did while going through my divorce was enough, not knowing the real healing and work would begin once I was in a relationship or dating. I now had the opportunity to see what all that past hurt and affliction really looked like on and in me—and, Chile, it was the ugliest thing I had ever seen.

I had to learn all over what it was to be in a relationship:

- •How to communicate.
- •How to properly handle conflicts and resolutions.
- •How to handle trust issues.
- •How to properly give in return what I asked for.
- •How to *love.*

You name it, and I had to relearn it. After a year of dealing with guy two, my taste for him started to change, and all the things I had been blind to were now clear as day.

I remember asking him what he wanted from me and why he liked me; he couldn't answer either question authentically or easily. I remember the moment I sent my final goodbye text and him half-tail calling me, wanting to know why I had decided to walk away from him. I also remember more so that there was no emotion, no fight, no sacrifice, no effort, or willingness to compromise on the issues we had when he called. He never once said he loved me or that this was not what he wanted, and his actions showed he was *definitely* not taking me or us seriously. *Eye-opening moment...*

What I learned was to trust my gut. I learned not to stay in a relationship or situation based solely on a person's potential but to instead see the reality of who they are. I also learned that sometimes we are our own worst enemy, and it's not always about what the other person does or has done to us but rather what we allow ourselves to keep signing

up for.   I even learned you should always stand firm in your
boundaries and your standards. This is where my healing began!

Live,

Love,

Laugh

"A FOOL VENTS ALL HIS FEELINGS, BUT A WISE MAN HOLDS THEM BACK."

-PROVERBS 29:11 NKJV

Shannon Stemley 65

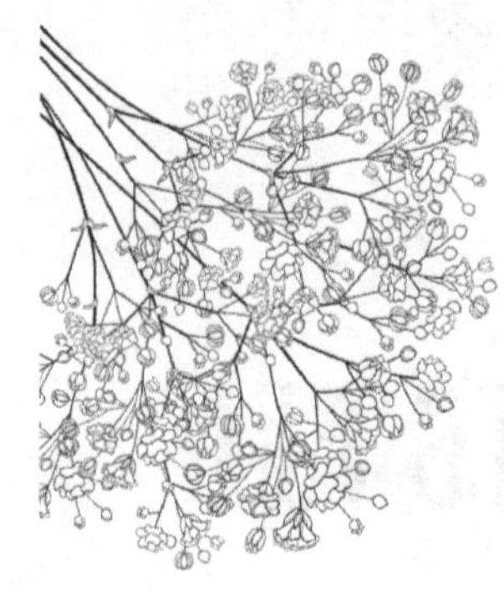

"YOU ARE WORTHY OF ALL YOUR HEARTS DESIRES."

-SHANNON STEMLEY

"WHEN GOD CLOSES DOORS LEAVE THEM CLOSED. HE HAS SOMETHING BIGGER AND BETTER IN STORE FOR YOU."

-SHANNON STEMLEY

Self- Reflect

Discovery

Sometimes we get scared in our singleness because we fear loneliness. More than that, we fear the thought of having to face ourselves. We fear doing the very thing we should be doing: healing, self-reflecting, loving ourselves, becoming self-aware, facing any denials, owning our flaws, and any problem areas. We fear being exposed, rejected, and the sneering looks from others if they were to see the authentic version of ourselves.

I, too, had a hard time accepting my singleness. I felt like not having someone to love or love me, not having someone to care for, and not having someone to create moments, memories, and experience life with made me incomplete. I measured my worth, value, and who I am as an individual solely on the presence or lack of others. I was the girl who was terrified at the thought of being alone and spending time by myself. I was even afraid of the thought of going out by myself. I felt like an idiot sitting in restaurants alone, walking through an event or festival alone, or going to the movies alone. It took time and lots of prayer, but now that fear is gone, and my alone time is what I look forward to. It's when I have the best use of time. My alone time is when I'm most relaxed, most at peace, and happiest. It is when I feel connected the most to myself and God.

Being alone in singleness forced me to see myself—I mean really see myself. I learned some of the most intimate things about who I am as a woman, a mother, a daughter, a sister, an aunt, a cousin, a niece, a granddaughter, a friend, a coworker, a neighbor, a wife (not just a girlfriend), and a woman of God. I had to learn how to create and be my own source of joy and happiness. I had to learn what I like and what I didn't like and what my triggers were. I had to rediscover myself and the things that were most important to me. Then I had to figure out the type of life I wanted for my children and me. Ultimately, I had to learn how to love me so that I could know the type of love I wanted and give healthy love the right way. I had to permit myself to feel and be human. I had to find the parts of me I lost in my marriage and rekindle my relationship with God.

What I discovered was this prison sentence called singleness was the biggest blessing ever! God uses this isolation period—singleness—as a moment for Him to mold you, push you, and allow you the room to grow into your purpose and into who you are designed and destined to be as an individual. You need to be happy and comfortable in your singleness so that you can go into a relationship as a *whole* individual, never losing sight of yourself. And when I mention relationship, I'm not just speaking of a romantic relationship but one of any origin. It would help if you never looked to others for validation, acceptance, or to fulfill your purpose or fill voids. All that credit belongs to the only one who can give either—GOD.

Live,
Love,
Laugh

"STOP TRYING TO PRAY
THE PERFECT PRAYER.
GOD SEES AND KNOWS
YOUR HEART EVEN WHEN
YOU CAN'T FIND THE
WORDS TO EXPRESS
WHAT'S IN IT."

–SHANNON STEMLEY

"I MISSED SO MANY THINGS GOD HAD FOR ME BECAUSE WHEN THEY CAME, THEY DIDN'T COME OR LOOK THE WAY I WANTED THEM TO COME OR LOOK."

—SHANNON STEMLEY

"IF YOU'RE TIRED OF PLAYING WITH CLOWNS, STOP SHOWING UP TO THE CIRCUS AND BEING A VOLUNTEER FOR THE ACT."
-SHANNON STEMLEY

Self- Reflect

Baggage Release

Always allow yourself room to grow and never feel bad for outgrowing the people in your life who choose to stay stagnant. I know it's easier said than done because as we elevate, we want those closest to us to come along for the ride. We want them to understand and take in the knowledge we seek, the experiences, and the feelings. Truth is, everyone in your life isn't called to travel every journey with you; I don't care how much you care about them or love them. When God shows us it's time to release certain people and things from our lives, we tend to ignore his Word—simply because what we want for ourselves, we want for others.

There were several times when I had a business idea or was experiencing a shift in my life, and I wanted to include my loved ones. I felt whatever God did in my life, I wanted to share with others. I eventually learned two lessons after years of hitting many stopping points or not being able to progress as I would have liked. One, some blessings come addressed with only your name on the envelope. When we try to add additional people to something only meant for us, God blocks it. He knows what his plans are for us and what is best for us. When we try to bring along someone else for the ride, we pretty much step in the way and hijack God's plans.

The second lesson I learned was to keep my mouth **closed**. Having the wisdom to know and understand that everybody who smiles in your face "ain't your friend" is key. There will definitely be people, even some of those close to you, who will pray for your downfall and failure. When we speak aloud about the good taking place in our lives, it activates the haters to start "preying against" you. It gives the enemy a head's up on how to start attacking you.

Keep your plans, goals, and blessings to yourself. Your business, no matter how big or small the information, is not for everybody to know. Some things are just worth holding onto, and when the time is right to let the world in on what's been taking place in your life, God will have already made it happen. We can literally keep ourselves stagnant by not being disciplined and obedient to His Word. *Grow!* And stop letting the guilt of others and their inability to expand hinder you from becoming the best *you!*

"IF GOD'S NOT IN IT, I DON'T WANT IT."

–SHANNON STEMLEY

"YOUR WORTH ISN'T DETERMINED BY SOMEONE ELSE'S ABILITY OR INABILITY TO SEE IT."
-SHANNON STEMLEY

"FOR THE SCRIPTURE SAYS, EVERYONE WHO BELIEVES IN HIM WILL NOT BE PUT TO SHAME."

-ROMANS 10:11 ESV

Self- Reflect

Self

Never let someone make you believe holding it down, being loyal, or a ride or die means accepting unhealthy toxic behavior. Real love will never leave you confused or unsure. Real love will never make you feel uneasy. It is not suffering; it is not conditional. Real love is not unfair or one-sided. It will never take you for granted nor take advantage of you. Real love will never punish you or betray you; it does not abandon you or lie to you. **Real love doesn't hurt.**

Never let anyone manipulate you into believing that being treated poorly equals love, loyalty, or respect. Again, you teach people how to treat you, and you teach them what's acceptable by what you allow. *Find* yourself, *accept* yourself, *love* yourself, and *be* yourself! Know your value and worth. More importantly, let it be seen by how you carry yourself. Speak affirmations and blessings over yourself. The perfect love is out there waiting for you. Stop settling and be patient!

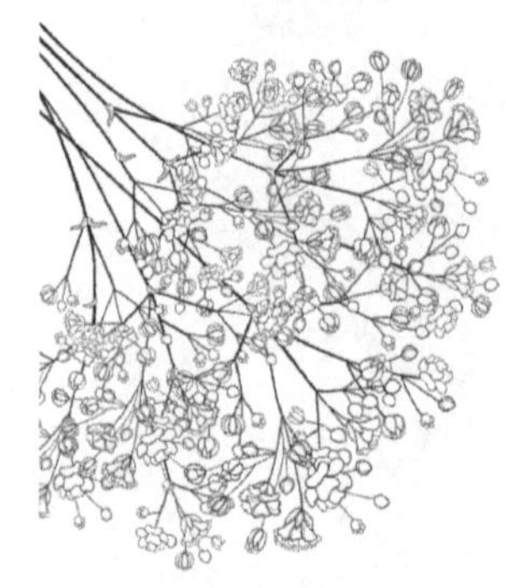

"YOU WILL NEVER WALK INTO WHAT GOD HAS FOR YOU IF YOU NEVER WALK AWAY FROM THE THING HE'S TRYING TO TAKE YOU FROM."

-SHANNON STEMLEY

"SITUATIONSHIPS *ARE* RELATIONSHIPS... JUST VERY UNHEALTHY, TOXIC ONES."

-SHANNON STEMLEY

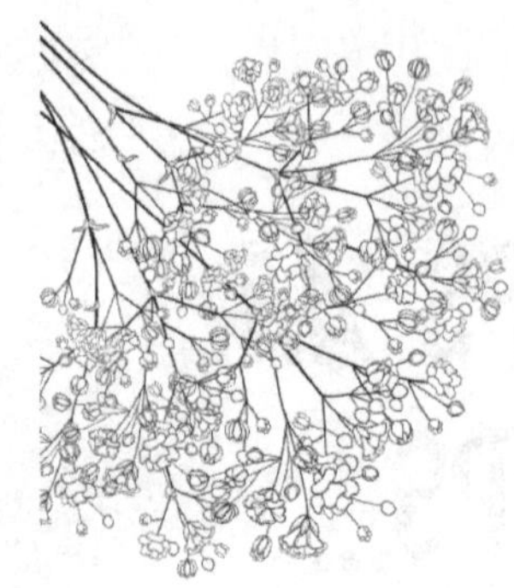

"IF YOU GONE REMEMBER, REMEMBER THE WHOLE THING."

-SHEILA SANDERS

Self- Reflect

God's Lesson #2

What I learned was, God will purposely allow us to enter situations and relationships intended only for a season, a reason, a lesson, or a lifetime. He pushes us into our purpose and destiny so that we can tap into our greatness.

God will purposely allow us to be blinded and naïve to dig ourselves so deep into a hole until we can seek only Him. Always on the other side of that season, reason, or lesson is a blessing so big and unimaginable, you can't even comprehend it. The key is, He's always waiting for us to do our part. God's patiently waiting for us to listen, to have and demonstrate faith, to trust Him, and then to step aside, allowing Him to be God. I can't even tell you how many times I have sat alone in silence and said, "Now wait a minute, Jesus. What is going on? What is it you want me to do, Lord? What lesson am I to get from this, and/or how is this going to better me?"

The thing about asking those questions is, you must first quiet yourself to hear Him speak. Secondly, know His answer won't come the way you expect it. It may even come through others, by words or actions. Next, we must be obedient to His Word. We can't ask Him to step in, and then when He gives us an answer, ignore it because it's not what we wanted or how we wanted it. Faith and trust in God are knowing He will never fail or forsake you.

God finds humor in hearing us tell Him what we plan for our lives. I honestly believe He sits in heaven, and the moment we say what *we* plan, He grabs His bowl of popcorn and says, "Okay, Shorty!" He always has a plan; Jeremiah 29:11 tells us just that, and His plan is the only plan. Trust the process and know God wants you to have all the goodness your heart desires. *Let Him work, okay, Shorty!*

"THE HEART OF THE DISCERNING ACQUIRES KNOWLEDGE, FOR THE EARS OF THE WISE SEEK IT OUT."

-PROVERBS 18:15

"SOMETIMES THE BEST RESPONSE IS NOT HAVING ONE."

-SHANNON STEMLEY

"WITH GOD ALL THINGS ARE POSSIBLE."

-MATTHEW 19:26

(ONE OF MY MAMA'S FAVORITES)

Shannon Stemley 95

Self- Reflect

Social Media Lies

I think a big mistake we all make is that we look at other people's lives and assume they have it all together. We think they have the perfect jobs, houses, cars, families, clothes, **relationships**, etc. We fantasize, wishing we had the same fortunes, not even taking the time to contemplate that we have no idea what that person has gone through to have those things; furthermore, what they are doing to keep them.

I can tell you from personal experience, judging people based on what you see from the outside is the shallowest and most ignorant thing you can do. I, myself, have been guilty a time or two of doing it. After tearful conversations with individuals who looked "together," I learned how naïve I had been in assuming they had a "perfect" life.

I also can speak as someone who was on the inside of the seemingly perfect life. Sometimes, wrapped inside that beautiful home is misery, hurt, depression, low self-esteem, disrespect, infidelity, brokenness, and God knows what else. Who determined that happiness and success were contingent on the image we presented to the world with material items and social media?

Live,
Love,
Laugh

"LET US NOT BECOME CONCEITED, OR PROVOKE ONE ANOTHER, OR BE JEALOUS OF ONE ANOTHER."

—GALATIANS 5:26 NLT

"WHEN THE TROUBLES OF THE WORLD WEIGH ME DOWN, I FIND COMFORT IN FALLING TO MY KNEES AND KNOWING I CAN CALL ON JESUS TO COMFORT ME AND CALM MY WORRIES."

-SHANNON STEMLEY

"THERE IS A CERTAIN LEVEL OF RESPECT, COMPASSION, PATIENCE, AND WILLINGNESS THAT COMES WITH UNDERSTANDING. GROWTH IS SEEKING TO UNDERSTAND INSTEAD OF ALWAYS WANTING TO BE UNDERSTOOD."

-SHANNON STEMLEY

Self- Reflect

The Mama In Me

We don't wake up suddenly knowing how to be the perfect parent. No one gives us a manual on parenting or holds our hands with complete guidance on how to handle every obstacle that will surely come our way. The truth is, most of us develop our parenting skills based on how our parents reared us, even if we didn't agree with every tactic.

For me, being the best mother I can be to my children has always been my priority. I never wanted them to experience the things I did as a child. I tried hard *not* to be my mother to my children. The hardest part of being an adult is unlearning and outgrowing the stuff you were taught, knowingly and unknowingly, by individuals who had no idea what they were doing either. For the most part, my kids had a life 10 times better than mine. I've made many mistakes in parenting, but who *hasn't?*

Where I lacked most was in my understanding at times with my children. Being set in your ways is a real thing, and sometimes we cling to the old, not even knowing we are. At times, I would expect my children to think, speak, and behave as I would—both as children and as adults. Where

I failed them was not always allowing them the room to be themselves. Now, I'm a firm believer that a child should be a child at all times. Children should be respectful, obedient, and, as I was taught, seen but not heard to a certain degree. After several incidents with my oldest, and after taking the time to stop and *listen* to my daughter explain how my demeanor can come off super-aggressive, what I learned was that I'm not always right just because I'm the parent.

"TRAIN UP A CHILD IN THE WAY HE SHOULD GO, AND WHEN HE IS OLD, HE WILL NOT DEPART FROM IT."

-PROVERBS 22:6 NKJV

"THANKFUL. GRATEFUL. BLESSED."

-SHANNON STEMLEY

"ALWAYS
MAKE
TIME FOR
YOU!"
-SHANNON STEMLEY

Self- Reflect

Feeling Myself

Letting go is hard. It's scary. It sometimes literally feels like death and a funeral. I had a hard time letting go, just like others do at times. In one specific specific situation, I was afraid that if I let go, I would never find that homie-lover-friend relationship I had with my ex in another man. I hadn't given myself enough credit in knowing that I *absolutely would* find everything I wanted and needed in the man God has for me. I had refused to acknowledge for so long how freaking awesome I really am! I remember when I stood in my bedroom, yelling to the top of my lungs, "Girl, you the shiggidy." (Not exactly the word I used, but growth has taught me that I don't need to cuss to express myself, but y'all know what I mean, lol!)

I looked in the mirror and reminded myself of the bad PYT I know I am:

1. I have a good job!
2. I'm starting my own business!
3. I have my own place!
4. I have my own car!
5. I have my finances in order!
6. I pay *all* my bills by myself, *and* I pay them on time, Boo!

Oh yeah… Ya' girl was crunk and all the way hype. Chile, I was feeling myself real hard that day, lol. Honestly, though, that's how I was supposed to feel all along. That was the exact attitude, courage, and self-love every other female and I should have daily.

As women, it's easy to get engulfed in a relationship and wrap ourselves around other people's needs and wants. Those nurturing instincts kick into gear, and we instantaneously want to do all and be all for a man, to show him how much we love and care for him. We spend so much of our time nurturing others. We forget to nurture ourselves in the same way sometimes, and we rarely receive the same time, effort, and energy we give back. We forget who we are and allow our identity to get lost in who we think we should be. We get engulfed in our *emotions* and begin to operate from that place.

The problem is when we operate from emotions, we lose self-control, and when we lose self-control, we allow ourselves to remain in seriously unhealthy relationships and situations. The beauty of knowing who you are in nurturing yourself is that you always know what you have to offer any relationship. You learn that letting go is sometimes the best thing you can do for both you and that person because holding on can create a circle of unhealthy and toxic behavior. You learn that you have options, too, so let go. You learn that sometimes people hold onto you, and you hold onto them, not because real, honest love is in the equation but instead because you're both available and convenient.

People will hold onto you (and you, them) wasting time, using each other as space-savers until what is genuinely wanted comes along. *Girl, let that go.* You will learn that God gives you the same 24 hours in a day, so using that time wisely and making time for those who make it for you is important, so let go. You learn that even in the hurt, disappointment, and disapproval, you will be **just fine**. You know that because you give, respond, respect, and love from a place of genuineness, the loss is never yours, so *let go and let God!*

"WHERE YOU
SEE LIMITS,
HE SEES
POSSIBILITIES."

-ANONYMOUS
(ONE OF MY MAMA'S FAVORITES)

"WE CAN'T SEE OURSELVES,
SO WE DON'T SEE
WHAT OTHER PEOPLE SEE;
WE SEE WHO WE THINK
WE ARE BUT NOT THE
VERSION THAT ACTUALLY
SHOWS UP."
-SHANNON STEMLEY

"IT'S EASY TO LOVE THE GOOD, BUT IF I CAN LOVE THE FLAWS AND PARTS YOU'RE ASHAMED OF, THEN LOVING YOU AS A WHOLE BECOMES TEN TIMES BETTER."

-SHANNON STEMLEY

Self- Reflect

____

____

____

____

____

____

____

____

God's Lesson # 3

Truth is, not every guy will treat you like the last guy or the one before him or the one before him. Not every guy is bad, broken, or has ill-intentions. At the end of the day, having discernment, trust, and faith is a must. Build *you!* Make *you* better! Love *you!* Set personal goals for yourself and work on improving you. Always follow your heart and intuition. Be good, and good will follow. Be accountable and take responsibility for what you allow into your life because realizing that *you* are in control is the best thing *you* can do.

When you understand that you control the people and things that come in and out of your life, you have a different perspective of life in general. *You* control the energy you receive. You also regulate your happiness and your career path. You are in control of the good and some of the bad in your life, both the acceptable and unacceptable behavior of others. You control how and when it's time to walk away. **You are in control!**

Never let the intentions of others make you behave in a manner you know, at the end of the day, you will regret and not be pleased with. Love in spite of and show up as the authentic version of you every time. Push forward, continue to love as passionate and endlessly as before, and don't make others suffer for the mistakes of the previous bad apples. Make it a habit of asking God to check your heart, mind, and soul so you operate from a place of goodness and pure authenticity. Gain self-control, so you're not operating from emotions. Stop trying to figure out how to get revenge or make others feel the hurt they caused. Believe and know God will take care of all your battles. The best thing you can do is concentrate on your own wholeness, happiness, and goals. *Glow up, baby!*

"THE TONGUE IS A POWERFUL
INSTRUMENT THAT CAN HURT,
HELP, OR REWARD YOU.
BE CAREFUL OF WHAT
YOU SAY OUT LOUD.
SOMETIMES WHAT YOU
THINK CAME FROM GOD
ACTUALLY CAME FROM THE DEVIL."
-SHANNON STEMLEY

"EVERY TIME
WE TELL GOD
OUR PLANS,
HE LAUGHS."

-SHANNON STEMLEY

"ANYONE WHO TRULY
LOVES AND VALUES
YOU WILL NEVER DO
ANYTHING TO MAKE
YOU FEEL UNLOVED
OR UNDERVALUED."
-SHANNON STEMLEY

Self- Reflect

False Love

Never give too much in the beginning. Some will fall in love with what you do for them before they ever see your heart and fall in love with it. I gave much of myself in the beginning to someone who didn't deserve any of me. The moment I realized I was all things for a person who was nothing for me did not feel good. I felt like a used-up dish rag. I thought about all of the things I did; none of the small or big gestures of love, kindness, and understanding were reciprocated—all of the time pouring into an empty cup and never being poured back into from the one-sidedness of the relationship we had grown into. How freaking unfair had he been? Most importantly, how unfair had I been to myself for allowing it?

Once I begin to stop doing all the giving, I noticed a shift in his attitude toward me. I saw him in his true form, and the snake slowly began to rear its head. I started to call him out more on his junk and voice my opinions more about how I wanted to be treated. I realized that no matter how often I voiced my concerns, hurt, or feelings, it all went unheard and unnoticed. He didn't care one way or another how he had treated me or how he made me feel. I was pouring into emptiness. He was only concerned about and in love with the

the benefits of having me, not so much with being *actually* committed to me.

I now know that taking your time and slowly giving pieces of yourself is especially important and that you don't have to explain or plead for the right person to love you and treat you right. Take your time; truly get to know the person. Get to know who they are at the core, not the representative they want you to see and know, or the potential of a person. The best part is, if it doesn't work or meet your standards, you have the choice to walk away.

I find no shame in saying it took me two failed attempts to get this right. I made the provisions I needed within myself by resetting, refocusing, and chin-checking myself. I re-evaluated and reinforced my boundaries and standards. I took the L's (losses and lessons), and I did not allow those circumstances to make me bitter, resentful, or cold-hearted. Life is all about lessons and the ability to learn from them, and this was one of mine, *but never again*, Hunty! Lesson learned. :)

"LOVE IS PATIENT, LOVE IS KIND.
IT DOES NOT ENVY, IT DOES NOT BOAST,
IT IS NOT PROUD.
IT DOES NOT DISHONOR OTHERS,
IT IS NOT SELF-SEEKING,
IT IS NOT EASILY ANGERED,
IT KEEPS NO RECORD OR WRONGS.
LOVE DOES NOT DELIGHT IN EVIL
BUT REJOICES WITH TRUTH.
IT ALWAYS PROTECTS,
ALWAYS TRUSTS, ALWAYS HOPES, ALWAYS
PERSEVERES. LOVE NEVER FAILS.
BUT WHERE THERE ARE PROPHECIES,
THEY WILL CEASE;
WHERE THERE ARE TONGUES,
THEY WILL BE STILLED;
WHERE THERE IS KNOWLEDGE,
IT WILL PASS AWAY."
-1 CORINTHIANS 13:4-8 NIV

"AND NOW THESE THREE REMAIN: FAITH, HOPE AND LOVE. BUT THE GREATEST OF THESE IS LOVE."

–1 CORINTHIANS 13:13 ESV

"LIVE EACH DAY WITH INTENTION."

– ANONYMOUS

ONE OF MY MAMA'S FAVORITES)

Self- Reflect

Love

I want someone who wants what I want. I want someone who can love me how I deserve to be loved and understands how I give love. Someone who can see me, and I mean really see all of me. Who can see all the good, the nurturing, the giving, the compassion, the thoughtfulness, the sassiness, and the kindness. The unconditional and limitless love I so freely give with every ounce of my heart.

I want someone who also cherishes and adores the bad, the flawed, the ugly, the not-so-nice at times, the stubbornness, and the times when I make it difficult to be loved. I want someone who sees my wants and needs and is attentive to those things. I want someone full of effort, patience, and understanding—someone who affectionately gives even when it requires sacrifice, compromising, and discomfort.

I want someone who can jump into this crazy thing called life with me while seeing and hearing my dreams, goals, and aspirations as I theirs, ready to steamboat forward to the life we so desire—together. A life full of laughter, **love**, family, joy, respect, loyalty, commitment, faithfulness, consistency, and happiness. Not perfect, but healthy and fair always. I want someone I can see the world with and embrace new cultures with; someone I can create everlasting moments, memories, and experiences with; someone who can love me through because I promise to give the same.

Live,
Love,
Laugh

"IT TAKES AN OPEN HEART TO HEAR WHAT YOU HAVE TO SAY."

-SHANNON STEMLEY

"BETTER IS OPEN REBUKE
THAN HIDDEN LOVE.
WOUNDS FROM A FRIEND
CAN BE TRUSTED,
BUT AN ENEMY
MULTIPLIES KISSES."
-PROVERBS 27:5-6 ESV

"LIVE, LOVE, AND LAUGH ALWAYS AND UNAPOLOGETICALLY."

–SHANNON STEMLEY

H. A. L. T.
NEVER REACT WHEN YOU ARE:

HUNGRY

ANGRY

LONELY

TIRED

— UNKNOWN

"A SOFT ANSWER TURNS AWAY WRATH, BUT A HARSH WORD STIRS UP ANGER."

-PROVERBS 15:1 NKJV

Uncomfortableness

(Unedited, Untouched, and Raw)

I was pushed into such an uncomfortable place by the revelation of the truth of a situation I was in and with an individual with whom I found myself entangled. The love. The care. The certainty of genuineness I thought was there and the realization of how blind, naive, gullible, and foolish I had been. All of these pushed me into an extremely uncomfortable place when a person who had no idea of the damage she was causing gave me the information she had. That uncomfortableness pushed me straight to God.

That uncomfortableness laid me right at the feet of God like a newborn baby crying in complete disbelief and utter shock. The uncomfortableness forced me to realize that I had placed a guy on a pedestal he had no business being on because, in my mind, there was absolutely no way my "friend" turned lover would ever do me that way. No way my "friend" could ever knowingly use me, hurt me, or lie to me. There was no way my "friend" could say he loves me and intentionally do what she was saying he had done. That Uncomfortableness forced me to question my judgement, loosely giving heart and rose-colored glasses that always sees the best in in folks, not the reality of who they indeed are. *Hmm.* The benefit of the doubt I like to give sure screwed me this time was my thoughts and feelings in this uncomfortableness. Why? How? AGAIN?

That uncomfortableness and sea of questions made me want to counsel with nobody but Jesus. I had made it way too far to let this situation bring me back 20 steps. Sitting in the uncomfortableness of it all, finding comfort in God, His word, His understanding, His counsel, His love, His peace, and His nonjudgmental view of me. Here is where I decided to turn that uncomfortableness into a comfortable life lesson I needed to learn. And boy-oh-boy, there are so many learned lessons that came from this whole situation. Looking back, I relive every conversation, every interaction with that person, and the moment I found myself in that uncomfortableness of knowing the truth, the truth of knowing he had played me and lied, straight up no chaser. I thank God for it all!

No more should've, would've, could've. It happened precisely the way God needed, wanted, and planned for it to happen. This was one of the many valleys I had to walk through in preparation for me shifting and leveling up to the next phase of life God has intended for me. There was no way God could take me to this new place in my life with all the baggage I had attached to me. Even that of my past. It was now that I understood that I had been tested my entire life in preparation for me being able to fully walk in my purpose and be able to handle all the adversities yet to come. And it's not that God didn't think I couldn't handle it before, but he had to equip me with another layer of armor. He had to groom me and make sure I was ready. God had to increase my knowledge, increase my strength, my ability to control my emotions and thoughts, my discernment, my wisdom, and my ability to handle the things that will surely come my way.

Just because He brought me through the trials and tribulations of my past and present, and just because I survived doesn't mean more trials won't come. They definitely will, but God needed to make sure I had the foundational strength, power, prayer, and know-how in fighting those tests; past, present, and future, not just in the natural but in the spiritual world. He needed to make sure I knew my most powerful weapon was Him, our Heavenly Father, and His word. He needed to make sure I never found myself dwelling in any uncomfortableness like that ever again.

There is no way, I mean, absolutely no way we can say we know God and have a relationship with Him but still allow something or someone He has total domain over to consume our hearts, minds, emotions, or spirit to a point where we forget who is in control. I immediately decided to walk with God, purposefully in the life He has planned for me, regardless of how I am viewed or judged. Let me tell you; I know it's hard because we form habits we don't' realize we create. We get comfortable in things we don't know we're comfortable in, and breaking away from those habits can be challenging to do. I understand now, the only way something like this could have made me uncomfortable to the core of my soul was by being so far removed from God and His word. Not even realizing how far removed I was, which allowed the enemy free range on my thoughts, actions, emotions, and words.

No. Nope. Nerp! Not allowing that to happen anymore and to ensure that it does not happen again, I had to stop trying to straddle the fence between God and the world.

Between loving God, living a life pleasing to Him, and being viewed as cool or hip. Between holding onto the old or stepping into the new. So, so many thoughts crowded my mind. But in the end, I rocked with God. The transition to finding my true self and embracing her is not as easy as I thought because finding your true self means not caring one way or another what anyone thinks or says about you. I don't care how tough or strong you are; you definitely think about other people's opinions from time to time. The Bible tells us God does not give us a spirit of fear. So, fear, doubt, or judgment cannot have any dominion over or within me. Amen! My soul purpose has become making sure I smell good always in the presence of God.

Making sure I am truly a living, breathing, walking example of His goodness. Heck, I want to make sure I smell good in the presence of whoever (and not that I don't smell good cause that Bond #9 keep ya girl right! but you know what I'm saying lol). I want to find comfort in being comfortable in all the uncomfortableness. That is real healing and happiness! (Smile) I keep telling people God has a sense of humor and an extraordinarily unordinary and unusual way of getting our attention and pulling us closer to him. Think about it (shoulder shrug). Whatever you do, *do not let your uncomfortableness win!*

Live,
Love,
Laugh

Self- Reflect

My Conclusion

Self... thank you for this journey. I've learned so much about who I am. My likes and dislikes, my standards, core values, highs, and lows, all while being with you. Through some difficult, hurtful, and even good experiences with you, I was able to discover parts of me I didn't know was there. I was forced to take a deeper look into myself and ravage through brokenness I didn't know still existed within me. I looked at the ugliest parts of me, face-to-face, and I had to decide which version would come out victorious, whether I would fight for who God designed me to be or fold to the false representative the world wanted to see.

Real talk... I had to decide on the woman I wanted to be and how I wanted to present *that* woman to my daughters as an example for them to look to. I strive daily to be the best example for my girls, other young girls, and any female struggling to see herself, to love herself, and to be no one other than herself. Healing is never an easy task, and I work every day to be better than I was the day before. It takes work, dedication, discipline, and devotion to self. It demands you to release people, places, and things you hold onto, hoping somehow, they heal the parts of you that you fear facing.

In my healing, I took great comfort in God and knowing He was exactly who He says He is; and He does exactly what He said He would do. I took comfort in knowing no matter how broken, destroyed, damaged, or undeserving of His love I thought I was, He loves me even when I don't love myself. I took comfort in plastering bible scriptures, quotes, affirmations, and the positive words I spoke to myself where I could see them as a constant reminder of the awesomely flawed woman I am. There is no perfect way to heal the hurt, the sadness, the grief, the pain, the unknown, or the brokenness. However, I took comfort in creating this book, hoping it would give another comfort in knowing someone else shares the same thoughts, feelings, and reactions.

This was my way of healing and rediscovering myself. I hope these brief experiences and feelings shared, coupled with the scriptures and quotes, bring you the comfort and peace they did me. Take care, Love Bugs, be easy on yourself. Be kind to yourself. Give yourself the exact love, care, and attention as you do others, and remember: manifesting the life you want (and its joys) all start with how you love and speak to yourself. It all starts with *you* and knowing the love of God!

XOXO,
Shannon

Live,
Love,
Laugh

"AS IRON SHARPENS IRON, SO A FRIEND SHARPENS A FRIEND."

-PROVERBS 27:17 NLT

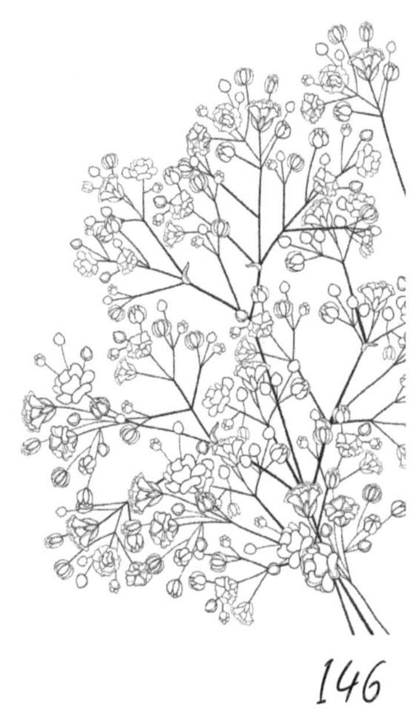

146

"THE LORD IS CLOSE TO THE BROKENHEARTED AND SAVES THOSE WHO ARE CRUSHED IN SPIRIT."

–PSALMS 34:18 NIV

My journey to wholeness began by making a conscious decision to change. I believe in the finished, redemptive work of Jesus Christ on the cross alone for the remission of all sins (past, present, and future) and eternal life!

Below are scriptures to meditate on as you make your decision to call on the name of the Lord.

- "All who call on the name of the Lord will be saved." (Romans 10:13)
- "I am the way, the truth and the life. No one comes to the Father but through me." (John 14:6)
- "When you declare with your mouth Jesus is Lord and believe in your heart God raised Him from the dead, you will be saved." (Romans 10:9-10)
- "For it is by grace you are saved through faith. It is not your own doing. It is the free gift of God. Not by works lest any man boast." (Ephesians 2:8-9)

Self- Reflect

About The Author

Shannon Stemley resides in Houston, Texas (H-Town), and the most esteemed title she carries is "Mom," mothering three beautiful souls (one son and two daughters). She is a Christian, an entrepreneur, and an advocate for self-love and helping others. Shannon uses her life lessons and experiences as inspiration to share her story in her first book, Moments, Memories, and Experiences.

Shannon never meets a stranger and carries a passion for giving back and helping in whatever way God directs her. As an entrepreneur, she has used her gifts of helping, communicating, and organizing to found and operate Admin Unlimited, LLC—a business solutions company providing virtual administrative and HR support to small businesses and entrepreneurs. Shannon is also a member and founder of the Bloom Book Club, where she gets to share her love for both reading and divulging in conversation on varying topics.

CPSIA information can be obtained
at www.ICGtesting.com
Printed in the USA
LVHW050526120121
676188LV00003B/130